Tom Thumb's Musical Maths

Developing maths skills with simple songs

Helen MacGregor

Maths consultant: Marion Cranmer

Illustrator: Michael Evans

A & C Black • London

Contents

Introduction
Teacher's notes

SECTION 3
Shape, space and measures

 ## SECTION 4
Mental arithmetic

For the children of Dog Kennel Hill Primary School

ISBN 978-0-7136-7295-4
First published 1998
Reprinted 1999, 2000, 2002, 2005, 2009, 2011
A&C Black Publishers Ltd
36 Soho Square London W1D 3QY
www.acblack.com

Author: Helen MacGregor
Maths consultant: Marion Cranmer
Editor: Ana Sanderson
Designer: Dorothy Moir, Peter Bailey
Illustrator: Michael Evans
Cover artist: Alex Ayliffe

Printed by Halstan Printing Group, Amersham, Buckinghamshire
This book is produced using paper that is made from wood grown in managed, sustainable forests. It is natural, renewable and recyclable. The logging and manufacturing processes conform to the environmental regulations of the country of origin.

Text © Helen MacGregor 1998
Illustrations © Michael Evans 1998
Cover artwork © Alex Ayliffe 1998

The author and publishers would like to thank the following people for their generous help during the preparation of this book:
Monica Ayton, Paul Gregory, Anna Lewis, Alasdair MacGregor, Sheena Roberts, Jane Sebba and Elaine Sutton.

Introduction

From an early age, children discover maths through music. They memorise number sequences through songs and chants, experience patterns through clapping and playing rhythms, and explore space in finger rhymes and action games.

Tom Thumb's Musical Maths is a collection of lively new songs to familiar tunes, which stimulate and complement the mathematical learning of young children. The songs offer imaginative ways to introduce and practise four areas of maths: **counting**; **number and algebra**; **shape, space and measures**; **mental arithmetic**.

The songs can be sung at different times and in a wide variety of situations. You can chant *Tom Thumb* during a spare two minutes; children can sing *Calculator heads* with families or friends; *The minibeast parade* can form part of a mathematical investigation into minibeasts, then be performed at assembly.

Most of all, I hope that everyone who sings these songs as they learn will enjoy the combination of maths and music!

Helen MacGregor

Teacher's notes

The following symbols are used in the teacher's notes:

 Indicates a basic description of how to use the song.

 Gives more maths with questions, investigations or extensions.

 Indicates a musical suggestion.

A summary of the maths focus of each song can be found in the bottom right hand corner of the page.

The first notes of each melody are indicated in the bottom left hand corner of the page. Melody lines are given at the back of the book.

1 Three around the world

Tune: Goosey goosey gander

We can count in English, you and me,
Sing all together, one, two, three.

We can count in Welsh, now, you and me,
Un, dau, tri; one, two, three.

pronounced *een die tree*

We can count in Spanish, you and me,
Uno, dos, tres; one, two, three.

oono doss tress

Counting in Swahili, you and me,
Moja, mbile, tato; one, two, three.

modja umbeelee tatoo

We can count in Chinese, you and me,
一 二 三 ; one, two, three.

ee err san

 This song is a useful starting point for work on number names with younger children. The children can make up their own verses for this song using languages relevant to them. They can also explore different ways of writing the numbers 1, 2 and 3.

 Add a musical sound at the end of each verse, e.g. *one, two, three.*

C   D   C   E   G   G   AG AC' G
We can count in Eng-lish, you and me

**counting 1 to 3
number symbols**

2 Food I like

Chant

Food I like,
One, two, three,
Chicken, cheese and cherry pie
Taste good to me.

Food I like,
One, two, three,
Cauliflower, carrots, beans
Taste good to me.

Food I like,
One, two, three,
Crisps, ice-cream, lemonade
Taste good to me.

☆ The children make up their own verses by choosing three different foods. They illustrate their choice of foods by drawing on photocopies of the plate opposite. Alternatively, they can use papier-mâché or clay food, or cut out pictures of food.

🚀 Choose a number of plates, each showing three different foods. How many different foods are there altogether?

🚀 Adapt this song for topic work relating to food. Change the last line to *are good for me* or *are bad for me*. The children suggest three healthy or unhealthy foods.

🚀 Investigate food sets (e.g. fruits, vegetables, breakfast foods, drinks) or other suggestions for sets (e.g. toys, games, sounds).

Food I like – *photocopiable plate*

3 Five wonky bicycles

Tune: John Brown's body

One wonky bicycle went riding round the town,
One wonky bicycle went riding round the town,
One wonky bicycle went riding round the town,
Then called another bike to cycle round.

Solo: *Sanjay*, follow on behind me,
Sanjay, follow on behind me,
Sanjay, follow on behind me,
We'll go 'bring bring' as we ride around.

Two wonky bicycles went riding round the town ...

Solo: *Rebecca*, follow on behind me ...

Three wonky bicycles went riding round the town ...

Solo: *Alex*, follow on behind me ...

Four wonky bicycles went riding round the town ...

Solo: *Maurice*, follow on behind me ...

Five wonky bicycles went riding round the town,
Five wonky bicycles went riding round the town,
Five wonky bicycles went riding round the town,
Until they started breaking down.

Solo: One went home without its back wheel,
One went home without its back wheel,
One went home without its back wheel,
That left four wonky bikes to ride around.

Four wonky bicycles went riding round the town ...
Solo: One went home without its front brakes ...

Three wonky bicycles went riding round the town ...
Solo: One went home without its pedals ...

Two wonky bicycles went riding round the town ...
Solo: One went home when it got rusty ...

One wonky bicycle went riding round the town ...
Then called another bike to cycle round ...

☆ One child mimes riding a wonky bicycle in verse one, then sings the chorus as a solo, choosing a friend to join in. Each new child chooses the next until there are five cyclists. The bikes then break down. The children can decide the order in which they break down – the first, fifth (or any of the other) bikes could break down first. Notice that the song has no end and can be used to introduce infinity – ask the children when it should end.

🚀 Investigate number facts. How many wheels, pedals or seats are there in each verse?

🎵 Each child can play a bell on joining the bike ride; each stops playing on breaking down.

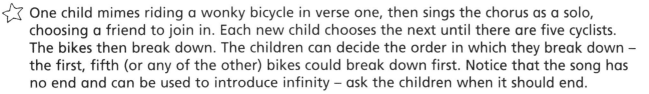

D   D   C B, D G   A   B B   B   A   G   1 to 5 5 to 1
One won-ky bi-cy-cle went rid-ing round the town   infinity

4 Five little seeds

Tune: Here we go round the mulberry bush

Five little seeds a-sleeping they lay,
A-sleeping they lay, a-sleeping they lay,
A bird flew down and took one away,
How many seeds were left that day?

Four little seeds a-sleeping they lay ...

Three little seeds a-sleeping they lay ...

Two little seeds a-sleeping they lay ...

One little seed a-sleeping it lay ...

No little seeds a-sleeping lay,
A-sleeping lay, a-sleeping lay,
A bird flew down but she didn't stay,
Because no more seeds were left that day.

☆ Five children curl up on the floor as seeds. The other children hold hands to form a circle around the seeds. During the first two lines of each verse, they walk clockwise around the seeds. Then they stand still as one child – the bird – flies into the centre, chooses a sleeping seed and takes it back to join the circle.

🚀 Start with a larger number of seeds. The bird chooses two seeds to eat each time. Alternatively, (s)he throws a die and takes away the number shown (e.g. *a bird flew down and took four away*). Can the children calculate in their heads the number of seeds left?

🎵 Accompany the song with maracas and tambourines. Five children play a steady beat, then shake their instruments in the air as the bird flies down. One child stops playing as the bird removes a seed.

F   F   F   F   A   C'   C'   A   F
Five lit-tle seeds a-sleep-ing they lay

5 to 0
subtraction

5 One banana

One button – adapted

One banana, two bananas, three bananas, four,
Five bananas, six bananas, seven bananas, more.
Seven bananas, six bananas, five bananas, four,
Three bananas, two bananas, one, no more!

☆ With this song you can
– use fingers to count up to seven and backwards from seven to zero
– enlarge the set of picture cards shown here for the children to shuffle then re-order, matching the sequence of numbers in the song
– use an enlarged number line to let children count up to seven, then backwards, while singing the song
– find other fruits to count (e.g. guava, pineapple, tomato, cucumber, green apple, ripe mango).

🚀 Sing the song, counting real objects (e.g. seashells, cubes and straws). Compare seven of each object to reinforce that although the size may differ, the number remains the same. The objects can be used to discuss comparative size (e.g the seashell is longer than the cube but shorter than the straw).

♫ Add clapping (or taps on instruments). Seven children stand in a line;
– on *one* the first child claps
– on *two* the second child joins in ...
– on *more* the whole class claps
– when counting backwards, all seven children clap on *seven*, then drop out one by one in reverse order.

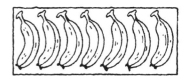

One banana –
photocopiable cards

C C C C D D D D   E   E   E E F
One ba-na-na, two ba-na-nas, three ba-na-nas, four

1 to 7 7 to 0
conservation of number

6 Five buzzy bees

Tune: Once I caught a fish alive

One, two, three, four, five,

Bees come buzzing from the hive,

Six, seven, eight, nine, ten,

Buzz *around* then back again.

Please tell me buzzy bee,
Why you buzz so busily.
'Peep in the hive to see,
We're making honey for your tea.'

☆ Use your fingers to count up to ten in the first verse.

🚀 Vary the last line of the first verse to explore different positions for the action. Change the word *around* to any of the following: *up high, down low, behind, in front, to the right, to the left,* and so on.

♫ The children play maracas as the bees buzz in verse one. They move the maracas as suggested by the words in the last line (e.g. *up high, down low*).

A   A   G   F   F
One, two, three, four, five

1 to 10
position

7 Mary up in a spaceship

Tune: Mary, Mary, quite contrary

All: *Mary, Mary*, sits in her spaceship,
We all count down from base.
With a ten, nine, eight, seven, six, five, four,
Three, two, one, zero, she's in space!

Mary, Mary, up in her spaceship,
Countdown for landing soon,
Solo: With a ten, nine, eight, seven, six, five, four,
Three, two, one, zero, hello moon!

☆ When the children can sing the first verse confidently, encourage the named child to sing the countdown in the second verse as a solo. (You can use an enlarged photocopy of the number line below – the named child can place a finger on it correctly while singing the countdown.)

♫ After verse one, a child plays a 'take off' sound effect by sliding a beater across the bars of a metallophone, going from the lowest to highest note (longest on the left to shortest on the right). After verse two, (s)he plays a 'landing' sound effect by sliding the beater from highest to lowest note (right to left).

0 1 2 3 4 5 6 7 8 9 10

Mary up in a spaceship – photocopiable number line

C' C' A A B♭ A B♭ G   G
Ma-ry, Ma-ry, sits in her space-ship

10 to 0
number line

8 Hickory digital clock

Tune: Hickory dickory dock

Hickory dickory dock,
I am a digital clock,
When you're asleep I start to bleep,
    Bleep, bleep, bleep,
What is the time on the clock?

☆ The digital clock has an alarm call which bleeps. (The bleep can be vocal, or played on a single chime bar, bell or buzzer.) A child – the clock – bleeps the correct number of times to communicate his/her chosen hour. (Pause after the third line of the song for the bleeps before singing the last line.) The other children – the sleepers – close their eyes to listen and, at the end of the song, say at what time they were woken.

🚀 Recognition of numbers. Make a digital clock with flip-over cards showing the hour (0.00 to 12.00). A child can bleep the number shown on the clock, revealing it to the rest of the class after they have answered.

0 1 2 3 4 5 6 7 8 9 10 11 12

Hickory digital clock – photocopiable digital numbers

E F G G A B C'
Hi-cko-ry di-cko-ry dock

0 to 12
digital numbers

9 Stamp and clap

Tune: Polly put the kettle on

Stamp your feet and clap your hands,

Stamp your feet and clap your hands,

Stamp your feet and clap your hands,

We'll stamp and clap.

Clap your hands and stamp your feet,

Clap your hands and stamp your feet,

Clap your hands and stamp your feet,

We'll clap and stamp.

☆ Divide the children into two groups – one to sing the song, the other to perform the actions shown. What do the children notice about the actions in each verse? (There is a pattern of two actions – stamp, clap – in the first verse, performed four times; the pattern is reversed for the second verse – clap, stamp.)

🚀 Explore patterns of sounds. Adapt the actions of the song to make a pattern of two stamps and claps:

Stamp your feet and clap your hands

What will the pattern be for the second verse? (Clap, clap, stamp, stamp.)

🚀 Try a pattern of three stamps and claps.

Stamp your feet and clap your hands

🚀 Invent and perform more patterns out of two new actions (e.g. *tap your knees and rub your tum*). Find ways of recording the patterns so that other children can perform them.

♪♪ Make up patterns with instruments,

e.g. *tap the drum and snake the bells.*

C' D' C' B♭ A F F
Stamp your feet and clap your hands

patterns

10 Piggy pairs

Tune: Tommy Thumb

 Piggy pairs, piggy pairs,

Where are you?

 Here we are,   here we are,

How do you do?

 Piggy pairs, piggy pairs,

How are you?

Oink, oink, snuffle, snuffle,

Fine, thank you.

☆ Perform the actions shown with or without finger puppets using two fingers of each hand.

🚀 The children discover new ways to order the pig sounds (e.g. *oink, snuffle, oink, snuffle*). How many ways can the pig sounds be ordered?

🚀 Sing about other animal pairs (e.g. *little ducks – quack, quack, wobble, wobble*), or two different farm, jungle or zoo animals (e.g. *lambs and cows – baa, baa, moo, moo; lion and bear – roar, roar, growl, growl*). The children use toy animals to investigate the patterns of sounds made by each pair of animals and compare the results.

🚀 Discuss other pairs of objects (e.g. socks, glasses, gloves). Investigate number patterns relating to pairs (e.g. the number of pairs of gloves needed for three children and the total number of gloves).

♫ Play instruments with the animal sounds,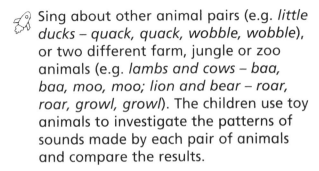

e.g. *oink, snuffle, oink, snuffle*.

E F G E F G
Pig-gy pairs, pig-gy pairs

patterns of 2
ordering

11 Greedy crocodile

Tune: What shall we do with the drunken sailor?

I am a greedy crocodile,
Sparkling teeth and charming smile,
Come too near and in a while,
You will be my dinner!

Solo: One, two, three, four, five,
One, two, three, four, five,
One, two, three, SNAP, SNAP,
Now I've had my dinner!

☆ In this action song, a child – the crocodile – decides how many children to eat from a line of five. In the third line of the chorus, the crocodile chooses a number of children to eat by replacing the numbers with a 'snap'. Can the other children say how many have been eaten?

♫ The crocodile can quietly tap a wood block on each number and loudly tap with each snap. Alternatively, (s)he can replace these words with quiet and loud sounds.

One two three SNAP SNAP

A A A A   A A D FA
I am a gree-dy cro-co-dile

subtraction

12 Cherries on a plate

Tune: The farmer's in his den

Cherries on a plate,
Cherries on a plate,
Two, four, six, eight,
Cherries on a plate.

Cherries on a plate,
Cherries on a plate,
Two, four, six, yum-yum,
Cherries on a plate.

Cherries on a plate,
Cherries on a plate,
Two, four, yum-yum, yum-yum,
Cherries on a plate.

Cherries on a plate,
Cherries on a plate,
Two, yum-yum, yum-yum, yum-yum,
Cherries on a plate.

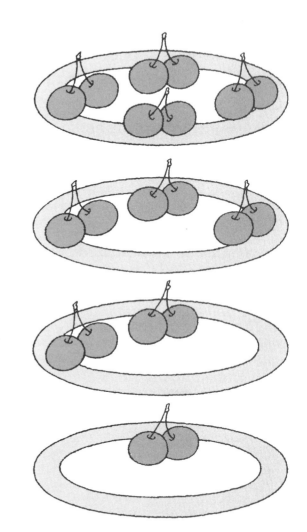

Cherries on a plate,
Cherries on a plate,
Plate is empty, there are no more,
Cherries on my plate.

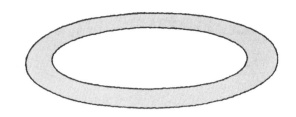

Cherries in my tum,
Cherries in my tum,
Yum-yum, yum-yum, yum-yum, yum-yum,
Cherries in my tum.

Cherries in my tum,
Cherries in my tum,
Two, four, six, eight,
Cherries in my tum.

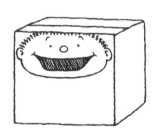

This song features counting in patterns of two and subtracting. These can be reinforced with a paper plate and pairs of cherries (real, paper, cloth or clay) which can be removed in each verse. Alternatively, draw a face on a cardboard box and cut out an open mouth, through which a child can place pairs of cherries. Put a pair of cherries in the box after each verse and ask how many cherries are in the tummy.

Either add a musical sound to the *yum-yums*, or replace them with sounds,

e.g. *two, four,*
(*yum-yum, yum-yum*)

G G A A G
Cher-ries on a plate

counting in 2s
subtraction

13 Babies in their cots

Tune: Jelly on a plate

Babies in their cots,
Babies in their cots,
One, two, three, four, five, six, seven, eight,
Babies in their cots.

They won't go to sleep,
They won't go to sleep,
Wa, wa, wa, wa, wa, wa, wa, wa,
They won't go to sleep.

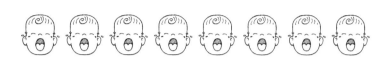

Sing a lullaby,
Sing a lullaby,
Sh, wa, wa, wa, wa, wa, wa, wa,
Sing a lullaby.

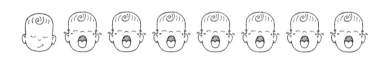

Pat them on the back ...
Sh, sh, wa, wa, wa, wa, wa, wa ...

Rock them in your arms ...
Sh, sh, sh, wa, wa, wa, wa, wa ...

Sing a lullaby ...
Sh, sh, sh, sh, wa, wa, wa, wa ...

(Continue making up more verses)

Last verse

Tiptoe down the stairs,
Tiptoe down the stairs,
Sh, sh, sh, sh, sh, sh, sh, sh,
Tiptoe down the stairs.

☆ Eight babies are soothed to sleep. Ask the children for suggestions of how to get the babies to go to sleep in order to make up more verses. Eight children can act out the song while the rest of the class perform appropriate actions for each verse.

🚀 Make eight double-sided baby face card discs, each showing a crying baby's face on one side and a sleeping baby's face on the reverse. Choose a child to arrange the pattern of faces before singing each verse of the song. Arrange them so that the pattern matches the song when reading the cards from left to right.

🚀 Use the cards to reinforce the concept of conservation of number (e.g. in both *sh wa wa wa wa wa wa wa* and *wa wa wa wa wa wa wa sh,* there are seven babies awake and one asleep).

🚀 Use the cards to devise different kinds of patterns (e.g. in twos – *wa wa sh sh wa wa sh sh,* or *sh sh wa wa wa wa sh sh*; symmetrical – *wa sh sh wa wa sh sh wa*). Can the children read the card patterns to sing new versions of the song?

🚀 In the last verse, instead of singing *sh* eight times, sing *wa* eight times, as though the babies have all woken up again. Then go back to the beginning of the song. Notice that this version of the song has no end and can be used to introduce infinity.

🎵 Substitute a sound on an instrument for each *wa* and a musical 'rest' (a silence) for each *sh*. Use the card patterns to play different combinations of sound and silent beats.

E G G G G
Ba-bies in their cots

patterns
conservation of number

14 One, two, three, together

Tune: In and out the dusky bluebells

One, two, three, together,

One, two, three, together,

One, two, three, together,

Clap your hands together.

One, two, three, together,

Four, five, six, together,

Seven, eight, nine, together,

Clap your hands together.

☆ Clap on the numbers only in verse one. How many claps were there altogether? Sing verse two to check the answer. Point out that the number pattern of three lots of three in verse one is the same as the number of claps.

🚀 In verse two, try omitting some of the numbers by 'silently' singing them (e.g * * *three together*, * * *six together*).

🚀 Divide the children into three groups and number them – one, two and three. Sing verse one with each group clapping only on its matching number. Can the children think of another way to perform this in three groups? (The groups could join in cumulatively – one group on *one*, two groups on *two*, and so on).

🚀 Try new number patterns (e.g. counting in twos – *two, four, six* ... or counting odd numbers – *one, three, five*, and so on).

♫ Replace the claps with sounds played on musical instruments (e.g. drums). Adapt the last line of each verse accordingly (e.g. *play the drums together*). Then repeat the above activities.

F	F	A	C'	A	F
One,	two,	three,	to-	ge-	ther

patterns of 3s

15 Baa baa maths sheep

Baa baa black sheep – adapted

Baa baa maths sheep, have you any wool?
Yes sir, yes sir, three bags full;
One for the master, one for the dame,
And one for the little boy who lives down the lane.

Baa baa maths sheep, have you any wool?
Yes sir, yes sir, six bags full;
Two for the master, two for the dame,
And two for the little boy who lives down the lane.

Baa baa maths sheep, have you any wool?
Yes sir, yes sir, nine bags full;
Three for the master, three for the dame,
And three for the little boy who lives down the lane.

☆ This version of *Baa baa black sheep* explores the pattern of the three times table.
Ask the children to illustrate the pattern of each verse with drawn or cut-out
paper bags. How would the song continue?

🚀 How many bags will the master, dame and little boy receive if there are 'no bags
full'?

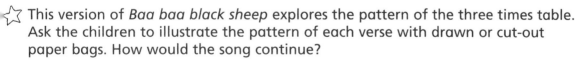

C C G G A B C'A G
Baa baa maths sheep, have you a-ny wool?

grouping

16 Bim bam bam

Tune: Pat a cake

Bim bam bam, bim bam bam, play the drum,
Bim bam bam, bim bam bam, we shall have fun,
Choosing a pattern that we like to play,
Bim bam bam, bim bam bam, tapping all day.

Tick tock tock, tick tock tock, knock on wood,
Tick tock tock, tick tock tock, sounds very good,
Choosing a pattern and getting it right,
Tick tock tock, tick tock tock, tapping all night.

☆ Teach the children the song and the sound patterns, playing them on imaginary bongos and two-tone wood blocks:

How many times is each pattern played in a verse? (Six times.)

🚀 Make up more patterns with the pairs of sounds (e.g. *bim bam bim, tock tock tick*). Think of other sound patterns that can be made on these instruments (e.g. *boom boom bang, tocky tocky tap*). Ask the children to record their patterns with pictures or writing.

♪♪ When the children can perform the song confidently, add the patterns played on real instruments.

C   E   G   C   E   G   G   F   F
Bim bam bam, bim bam bam, play the drum

patterns

17 Ten little snowfriends

Chant

 Five little snowmen going for a walk,

Five little snowmen stopped for a talk,

 Along came five little snow-women, then,

 They all danced together and that made ten.

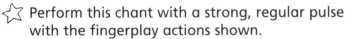 Ten little snowfriends danced all night,

Under the moon and the stars so bright,

Early next morning up came the sun,

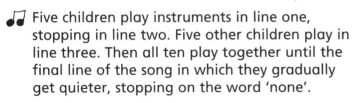 Warmed all the snowfriends, so then there were none!

 Perform this chant with a strong, regular pulse with the fingerplay actions shown.

 Either make paper snowpeople or act out the chant. Find other ways of arranging the ten snowfriends. Use pictures or ten children to work out the different arrangements.

♫ Five children play instruments in line one, stopping in line two. Five other children play in line three. Then all ten play together until the final line of the song in which they gradually get quieter, stopping on the word 'none'.

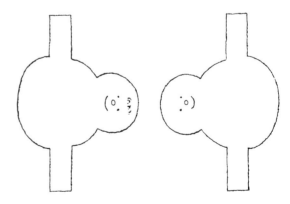

Photocopiable templates – for finger puppets, or lines of snowmen or women.

5+5 10-10
patterns

18 The minibeast parade

The ants came marching – adapted

The ants came marching two by two,
    Hurrah, hurrah,
The ants came marching two by two,
    Hurrah, hurrah,
The ants came marching two by two,
In summer they grew wings and flew,
And they stamped their feet and flapped their wings
In the minibeast parade.

The ladybirds crept in four by four,
    Hurrah, hurrah,
The ladybirds crept in four by four,
    Hurrah, hurrah,
The ladybirds crept in four by four,
Their little feet made no sound on the floor,
And they stamped their feet and flapped their wings
In the minibeast parade.

The crickets came hopping six by six ...
All of them up to their jumping tricks ...

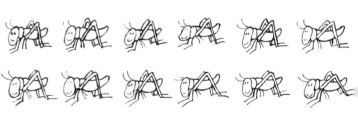

The beetles came scuttling eight by eight ...
Hurrying so that they wouldn't be late ...

The bees came buzzing ten by ten ...
Buzzing this song again and again ...

☆ For the purposes of the following activities, *two by two* is interpreted as two groups of two, *four by four* as two groups of four, and so on, so that the number of creatures increases by four in each verse.

🚀 Illustrate the minibeasts and calculate the total number in each verse. With this information, draw up a chart and work out the relationship between the verses (four, eight, twelve, sixteen, twenty). Ask how many more minibeasts there are in each verse.

🚀 Divide twenty children into two groups of ten. Two children from each group (i.e. four children altogether) accompany the first verse, marching their hands on alternate knees (left, right, etc). For the second last line, they do the actions suggested by the words. Add two more children from each group to the next verse, and so on, until all twenty children are accompanying the final verse. Work out how many children in the class are left over. How many more verses are needed for everyone in the class to be included in the song? Make up more verses as required. Any remaining group of fewer than four children can accompany the whole song with footstep sounds played on wood blocks.

🎵 Play the beat with each verse, choosing instrumental sounds to represent the creatures and their movements (e.g. castanets played quietly for the ants).

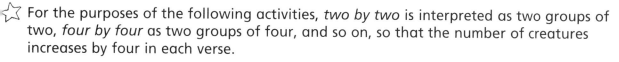

B♭ B♭ E E F♯ G F♯ G
The ants came march-ing two by two

grouping

19 Centipede and millipede

Tune: Jack and Jill

Centipede has lots of legs
To climb up garden walls;
They stop him from falling off,
He counts them as he crawls.
Chant: Zero, ten, twenty, thirty, forty, fifty, sixty, seventy, eighty, ninety,
one hundred!

Millipede has even more,
And they give her the blues;
It takes her all the day and night
To put on all her shoes.
Chant: Zero, one hundred, two hundred, three hundred, four hundred,
five hundred, six hundred, seven hundred, eight hundred,
nine hundred, one thousand!

Centipede has lots of legs
To climb down garden walls;
Sometimes he goes back legs first,
He counts them as he crawls.
Chant: One hundred, ninety, eighty, seventy, sixty, fifty, forty, thirty,
twenty, ten, zero!

Millipede has even more,
And they give her the blues;
It takes her all the day and night
To take off all her shoes.

Chant: *One thousand, nine hundred, eight hundred, seven hundred,*
six hundred, five hundred, four hundred, three hundred,
two hundred, one hundred, zero!

☆ This song features chants for counting in tens and hundreds. Practise the first two verses several times before introducing verses three and four which feature counting backwards.

🚀 Make a wall frieze to show what a centipede with one hundred legs looks like. Ask small groups of children to draw and cut out sets of ten legs, then add each set to one segment of a long centipede. How many segments will the centipede need? (Note that centipedes and millipedes do not actually have a hundred or a thousand legs! Centipedes have one pair per body segment, millipedes have two pairs per segment.)

🚀 Draw attention to *centi-* and *milli-*. Think of other words with these beginnings (e.g. centimetre, millimetre, centilitre, millilitre, century, millennium).

E   E   E   E   A   A   A
Cen-ti-pede has lots of legs

0 to 100   10s   0 to 1,000   100s
100 to 0   1,000 to 0

20 Circle

Tune: Round and round the garden like a teddy bear

Round and round the circle,
Draw one in the air,
Stop, look, find one,
Circles are everywhere.

☆ This simple fingerplay encourages children to recognise circles in their environment. Perform it with the actions suggested.

🚀 Discuss curved and straight edges. Which shapes have only straight edges? Only curved edges? A mixture?

🚀 After singing the song, ask a child to describe the position of a circle without pointing to it (e.g. it is above the door; it is next to the bookshelf). Can the other children identify the circle?

♫ Add a 'circular' sound to line one. Ask a child to trace a fingertip or the head of a beater 'round and round' the skin of a tambour or the edge of a cymbal.

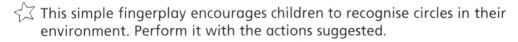

C   D   C   E   G   G
Round and round the cir-cle

circles
shape properties

21 Triangle

Tune: Three blind mice

Tri - an - gle, tri - an - gle,

Three straight sides, three straight sides,

It isn't a circle, it isn't a square,

You can see triangles everywhere,

You can even hear if you listen with care

A triangle. TING!

 This fingerplay teaches the properties of a triangle. At the end, the children can point to a triangle in the room. Encourage them to look for different kinds of triangle.

 What else does a triangle have three of, not mentioned in the song?

 Use a triangle instrument to demonstrate the shape. Then ask individual children to play the triangle. Can they play a single triangle tap at the end of the song?

 To reinforce the idea of three, add three triangle taps to the first two lines of words – one on each side of the triangle. Play this as an ostinato (repeating pattern) accompaniment throughout the song.

E D C E D C
Tri-an-gle, tri-an-gle

22 Square

Tune: Frère Jacques

Find four corners, find four corners,

Sides the same, sides the same,

Put them all together, put them all together,

Square's my name, square's my name.

Can you see me? Can you see me?
Anywhere? Anywhere?
Hiding in the *classroom*, hiding in the *classroom*,
Over there! Over there!

This song describes squares and asks the children to search for them in the classroom. If you wish, replace the word *classroom* in verse two with *picture*, *playground*, or another environment.

This song can be taught as an echo song. When the children know it well, they can sing it in two groups, taking turns to sing the lines first or second.

F G A F F F G A F
Find four cor-ners, find four cor-ners

**square
shape properties**

23 Which shapes?

Tune: Oranges and lemons

All: Which of these shapes can you see in our classroom?
Triangle, rectangle, circle or square?

Solo: I see a *circle* here in our classroom.

All: *Sam* found a *circle*, now please show us where!

☆ This game song asks individual children to find one of four simple shapes.
Everyone sings lines one, two and four, and a chosen child sings line three as a
solo. At the end of the song, (s)he may point to the identified shape or describe
its position (e.g. over the door, on the table, behind me) so that the rest of the
class can find it.

♫ Accompany the song with a drone: play the notes C and F on chime bars during
lines one and two, and C and G during lines three and four.

C' A C' A F GA B♭ G C' A F
Which of these shapes can you see in our class-room?

finding shapes
positional language

24 Sea shapes

Tune: A sailor went to sea

Group 1: A sailor went to sea, sea, sea.
Group 2: So what shapes did he see, see, see?
Group 1: Well, all that he could see, see, see,
          Was the shape of the big ship's wheel.

          ... Was the shape of the flapping sails.

          ... Was the shape of the captain's log.

          ... Was the shape of the old ship's flag.

Group 2: A pirate went to sea, sea, sea.
Group 1: So what shapes did she see, see, see?
Group 2: Well, all that she could see, see, see,
          Was the shape of the treasure map.

          ... Was the shape of the mark on the map.

          ... Was the shape of the hole in the sand.

          ... Was the shape of the golden coins.

Sea shapes – *photocopiable illustrations*

☆ Photocopy and enlarge the illustrations so that the children can identify the shapes in each verse. (The children can make their own versions of the two pictures and add more shapes.)

🚀 Extend the song by asking the children to make up new verses, using three-dimensional shapes (e.g. a treasure chest – cuboid; the pirate's glass eye – sphere; telescope – cylinder).

♫ Add watery sounds as an accompaniment to the song (e.g. slosh water in a plastic bottle or gently roll a maraca). Play the note C on a chime bar with each sea/see word.

G C' G A G E G G
A sai-lor went to sea, sea, sea

identifying 2D shapes

25 Mystery bag

Tune: This old man

2D SHAPES

Mystery bag, what's inside?
What's the shape you try to hide?
It's a circle, triangle, rectangle or square,
Feel the shape, describe what's there.

3D SHAPES

Mystery bag, what's inside?
What's the shape you try to hide?
It's a cube or cuboid, pyramid or sphere,
What is it? We want to hear!

 For this game song, you will need a cloth bag and the shapes mentioned in the song.

Secretly place one flat shape in the bag and sing verse one. Invite a child to feel inside and, without looking, describe the properties of the shape (s)he can feel (e.g. three corners, three straight sides). The child shouldn't name the shape. The rest of the class identify the shape being described before it is revealed. Repeat the game with another shape. Use the second verse to play the game with three-dimensional shapes.

 Adapt this game for pairs of children. Take two bags and place one set of either the two-dimensional or three-dimensional shapes in each. One child feels inside a bag and describes, without naming, to a partner, the properties of the shape (s)he has found first. The partner feels for the matching shape in the second bag and names it. Both children take the shapes out of the bags to compare and check.

   A   F♯   A   A   F♯ A
Mys-tery bag, what's in-side?

2D and 3D shapes

26 Sun, stars and moon

Tune: Pease pudding hot

Start of the day,
Sun rising high,
Circle of yellow light
In the sky.

End of the day,
Sun setting low,
Red semi-circle
Brings a glow.

Start of the night,
Stars twinkling high,
Each point shines brightly
In the sky.

End of the night,
Watching the moon,
Crescent of white light
Will fade soon.

Start of the day ...

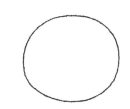

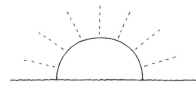

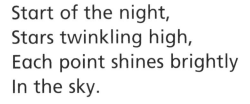

Discuss with the children the following words which describe time – dawn, morning, day, evening, night. Teach the song and ask how many hours the song describes before the first verse is sung again. When should the song end?

Discuss how the sun, a star and the moon are represented when drawn. What are these shapes like? How do they relate to the actual shapes and the shapes we see from earth?

How does the shape of the moon change?

Cut out a selection of star shapes and let the children sort them into sets according to the number of points. What is the smallest number of points a star can have? Make a graph to show the results.

Use a soft beater to play a cymbal getting gradually louder in verse one and quieter in verse two. Choose instruments to represent the stars and the moon in the next two verses respectively.

C C D E
Start of the day

shapes time
handling data

27 Three ducks

Tune: Twinkle, twinkle, little star

Watch the ducks and you will see,
They are waddling, one, two, three.
First the smallest leads the line,
Middle-sized duck thinks second place is fine,
Biggest duck is third, you see,
They are waddling, one, two, three.

 This song introduces order and size, and can be illustrated with three toy ducks of clearly contrasting sizes.

 Work on order. Change the order of ducks to sing a new version of the song, e.g.
... First the biggest leads the line,
Smallest duck thinks second place is fine,
Middle-sized duck is third, you see ...
Which duck is last? Place the toy ducks in the wrong order, then sing the song. Can the children spot the mistake and, at the end of the song, re-order the toy ducks?

 Work on size. Using a photocopier, enlarge or reduce pictures of ducks to cut out. Start with obviously different sizes for each set, progressing to sets which are closer in size as the children become more able to check. Find ways to check size (e.g. measuring with bricks or centimetre cubes). Try estimating the sizes (height/length) of different ducks in bricks or centimetre cubes.

 Play a loud, medium loud and quiet sound on an instrument to represent the three duck sizes (big, middle-sized and small). Make a sequence using the three sounds; the children place the ducks in the corresponding order.

D D A A B B A
Watch the ducks and you will see

order
size

28 Favourite toys

Tune: The wheels on the bus

A yoyo on a string rolls up and down,
Up and down, up and down,
A yoyo on a string rolls up and down,
That's my favourite toy.

A jack-in-a-box pops out then in,
Out then in, out then in,
A jack-in-a-box pops out then in,
That's my favourite toy.

A spinning top spins round and round ...

A garden swing moves forward and back ...

A kite in the sky flies far and near ...

A racing car turns left and right ...

A sledge slides down from top to bottom ...

☆ This song uses vocabulary describing position. Make sure that the children have enough space to move their whole bodies appropriately with the words of each verse.

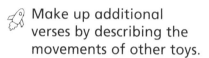 Make up additional verses by describing the movements of other toys.

♫ Choose a musical sound to represent the movement of the toy in each verse (e.g. slide a beater up and down the bars of a xylophone for the yoyo rolling up and down; play a drum loudly then quietly for the jack-in-a-box popping out then in).

C F F F F F A C' A F
A yo-yo on a string rolls up and down

position

29 The hokey cokey

The hokey cokey – adapted

You put your right arm up,
You put your right arm down,
Up, down, up, down,
Shake it all around;
You do the hokey cokey
And you turn around,
That's what it's all about.
    Oh, the hokey cokey,
    Oh, the hokey cokey,
    Oh, the hokey cokey,
    Knees bend, arms stretch, jump up and down.

You put your left arm up,
You put your left arm down,
Up, down, up, down,
Shake it all around ...

You take one jump forwards,
You take the next jump back,
Forwards, back, forwards, back,
Don't make the floorboards crack ...

You move a half turn left,
You move a half turn right,
Left, right, left, right,
You move all day and night ...

You move a quarter turn left,
You move a quarter turn right,
Left, right, left, right,
You move all day and night ...

This traditional dance song has been adapted to include some extra mathematical instructions. You and the children can think of more. (E.g. investigate what happens if the children move a quarter turn left, then three quarters turn right. Are they back where they started? Which way are they facing now? Why?)

Add instruments to the chorus. Choose a long sound (e.g. shaken tambourine) to play with the first three lines of the chorus:

Oh, the hokey cokey

Then tap the rhythm of the words of the last line:

Knees bend, arms stretch, jump up and down.

D   E   D   G   G   G
You put your right arm up   **position**

30 Footsteps

The grand old Duke of York – adapted

Oh, the grand old Duke of York,
He had ten thousand men,
They measured their steps to the top of the hill,
And they measured them down again.
Oh, one and two and three,
And four and five and six,
And seven, eight and nine, keep counting,
Ten, eleven, twelve!

Oh, the grand old Duke of York,
He had ten thousand men,
They measured their steps to the top of the hill,
And they measured them down again.
And when they were up, they were up,
And when they were down, they were down,
And when they were only halfway up,
They were neither up nor down.

☆ Act out the first verse with the children starting from the same position (e g. a line marked on the floor). What happens if they all take twelve footsteps, choosing their own length of stride? Can they work out why they have not all travelled the same distance? What should they do to travel the same distance when they take twelve steps?

🚀 Sing the second verse. Draw a picture of the hill and work out where to place the numbers one to twelve representing the footsteps. If the men take twelve footsteps to reach the top, how many will they need to get back down? Halfway up? From the top to halfway down? From the beginning, up and halfway down again?

B A G D B, D G
Oh, the grand old Duke of York

measures

31 Recipes

Tune: Yankee Doodle

WITCH'S RECIPE
Half a kilo of mouldy cake,
Mix with twenty weasels,
Add a dozen wizard's teeth,
A spell to cure the measles!
    Half a litre of fresh toad's blood,
    A pair of smelly socks,
    Add a kilo of wiggly worms,
    A cure for chicken pox!

HUMAN'S RECIPE
Break two eggs into a bowl,
Add two large spoons of flour,
Stir in half a pint of milk,
And leave for half an hour.
    Pour some mixture in the pan,
    Doesn't it smell yummy,
    Fry it, toss it, no mistake,
    A pancake for your tummy!

☆ Explore weights and measures using the quantities of ingredients in each of the recipes.

🚀 The witch's recipe. Make a painted papier-mâché cake when the children have estimated the required sizes by investigating packaging and real cakes. Make weasels, socks and wizard's teeth from paper. Add food colouring to water for the toad's blood and use coloured, cold spaghetti for the worms.

🚀 The human's recipe. Compare this pancake recipe with others in recipe books. What other measures are used for the flour and milk? What units of measurement are used for milk sold by the milkman and in the shops? Do any of the recipes use metric measures for milk? Compare half a pint of milk with half a litre of toad's blood from the witch's recipe.

G G GA A B G   B A
Half a ki-lo of moul-dy cake

measures

32 Supermarket shop

*Tune: **One man went to mow***

Going to buy some food
At the supermarket,
One tin of baked beans,
Put it in the basket.

Going to buy some food
At the supermarket,
One tin of baked beans and a bag of rice,
Put them in the basket.
    ***Teacher:** How many items are in the basket now?*

Going to buy some food
At the supermarket,
One tin of baked beans and a bag of rice,
    and a box of eggs,
Put them in the basket.
    ***Teacher:** How many items are in the basket now?*

... and a loaf of bread ...

... and a carton of milk ...

☆ Set up a classroom shop with various items to buy. Sing the song as individual children choose an item to put in the basket for each verse. (Alternatively, go to the local supermarket and sing as you collect!) The children may want to extend the numbers beyond five or shop for particular types of food (e.g. fruit or vegetables only).

🚀 Compare the size and shape of a variety of packaging. Which shapes will fit most easily into the basket? How many boxes of cereal does it take to fill the basket? How many tins of beans?

🚀 Collect increasing numbers of items in each verse, e.g:
   ... one tin of baked beans ...
   ... two tins, one tin of baked beans ...
   ... three tins, two tins, one tin of baked beans ...
After each verse, ask how many tins of beans there are in the basket.

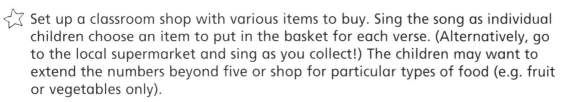

F♯ F♯ F♯ F♯ F♯
Going to buy some food

shape
counting

33 Calculator heads

Tune: She'll be coming round the mountain

We have all got calculators in our heads,
We have all got calculators in our heads,
We have all got calculators, all got calculators,
All got calculators in our heads.

Singing izzy wizzy busy buzzing brains,
Singing izzy wizzy busy buzzing brains,
Singing izzy wizzy busy, izzy wizzy busy,
Izzy wizzy busy buzzing brains.

We can calculate the answer in our heads,
We can calculate the answer in our heads,
We can calculate the answer, calculate the answer,
Calculate the answer in our heads.

Teacher:	*Children:*
Singing two add two makes –	*four!*
Singing two add two makes –	*four!*
Singing two add two, two add two,	
Two add two makes –	*four!*

We can calculate the answer in our heads ...

Teacher:
Singing three times three equals –

Children:
nine ...

We can calculate the answer in our heads ...

Teacher:
Singing twenty minus fifteen leaves –

Children:
five ...

This quiz song can be used for mental calculations at any level. Sing it to individuals, small groups or the whole class to practise mental addition, subtraction, multiplication or division. Encourage the children to supply the answer at the end of each line. Make up your own words to give calculations at the appropriate level for your children, reinforcing a wide range of mathematical language (e.g. *five add five equals 'ten'; take four from five, that leaves 'one'*).

Sit in a circle. Sing the choruses together, then one by one, the children make up a sum for everyone else to calculate. They might suggest some complex calculations. Discuss different ways of finding the solutions.

The children could use beans or cubes to calculate the answers as the sum is sung.

C D F F F F D C A, C F
We have all got cal-cu-la-tors in our heads

**mental arithmetic
mathematical language**

34 Double dumplings

Tune: Diddle diddle dumpling

DOUBLING NUMBERS
Double, double dumpling, come with me,
Have a slice of cake and a cup of tea.
Choose a number, you will see,
We can double numbers easily.

FRACTIONS
Double, double dumpling, come with me,
Have a slice of cake and a cup of tea.
Choose a fraction, you will see,
We can name fractions easily.

☆ Investigate doubling numbers with verse one. Make dumplings from papier-mâché or circles of cards and place them on a paper plate. Write a selection of numbers to be doubled on cards. Sit the children in a circle with the plate of dumplings in the centre and the number cards face down. Pass an empty plate around the circle as the children sing verse one together. At the end, the child who is holding the plate turns over a number card from the centre and takes double that number of dumplings. If the child is unsure of how many dumplings to take, (s)he can check by taking the number indicated by the number card, then match it with an equal number before counting the total.

🚀 Investigate fractions with verse two. Make paper cakes divided into slices – halves, quarters, and so on. Place the cake slices in the centre of the circle. As before, pass an empty plate around the circle as the children sing verse two together. At the end, the child who is holding the plate chooses a slice of cake and identifies the fraction.

G	G	G	G	F♯	F♯	G	G	E
Dou-ble,		dou-ble	dump-ling,			come	with	me

doubling numbers
fractions

35 Hippity hop

Tune: Pop goes the weasel

Hippity hop to the barber's shop
To buy a stick of candy,
One for you and one for me,
And one for sister Mandy.
    Teacher: *How many did you buy?*

Hippity hop to the ice-cream shop
To buy a lemon lolly,
Two for you and one for me,
And one for Uncle Jolly.
    Teacher: *How many did you buy?*

Hippity hop to the grocer's shop
To buy a juicy melon,
Two for you and two for me,
And one for baby Helen.
    Teacher: *How many did you buy?*

☆ This song can be used to practise simple or more advanced mental addition. Ask the children to work out the total number of items bought in each verse. To extend the calculations, change the numbers. Can the children add three lots of five, ten, one hundred or one thousand? Can they calculate mixed numbers (e.g. two, seven and one)?

🚀 Give a total number of items which is a multiple of three. Then sing the song, sharing the items equally. Use different methods to work out how many each will get. (E.g. how many groups of three can be made if the total is nine? What is the result if nine items are shared out one at a time – one for you, one for me, one for baby Helen, and so on?) Give a total which is not a multiple of three and use the same methods to work out how many items each person will get.

D D F♯ E   E G F♯ A F♯   D
Hip-pi-ty hop to the bar-ber's shop

mental arithmetic

36 Sing a song of pocket money

Tune: Sing a song of sixpence

Sing a song of one pound,
A pocket full of money,
Standing in the newsagent's,
My brain is feeling funny!
Fifty pence a comic,
That's what I'll have to pay,
So how much change will I have left
To spend another day?

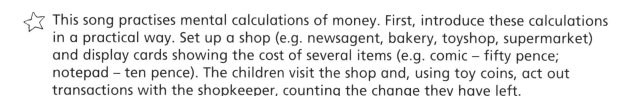 This song practises mental calculations of money. First, introduce these calculations in a practical way. Set up a shop (e.g. newsagent, bakery, toyshop, supermarket) and display cards showing the cost of several items (e.g. comic – fifty pence; notepad – ten pence). The children visit the shop and, using toy coins, act out transactions with the shopkeeper, counting the change they have left.

Progress on to singing this song and calculating problems set by you or other children. To develop this activity further, change the unit of money in the first line (e.g. *sing a song of ten pence*, or *ten pounds*, or *two pounds*).

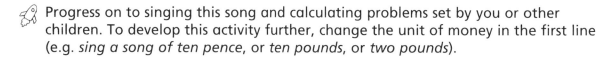 Play a 'pocket money' beat with the song by shaking a cloth purse or bag containing a few pennies (or metal washers).

A G♯ F♯ E A C♯
Sing a song of one pound

mental arithmetic
money

37 Tom Thumb

Chant

All: Tom Thumb, Tom Thumb,
What's the answer to this sum?

Teacher: *Four minus three –*
Katie: *One.*

Teacher: Your answer's right, there's no doubt,
All: Tell us how you worked it out.

All: Tom Thumb, Tom Thumb,
What's the answer to this sum?

Teacher: *Two times four –*
Rashid: *Six.*

Teacher: Good try, not quite,
All: Let's all help to get it right.

This simple chant can be used at any time, anywhere, to pose mental arithmetic sums of any level of difficulty. At the end of Tom Thumb's chorus, set a problem and choose a child to solve it. Following the answer, chant the appropriate response (*your answer's right, there's no doubt* for a correct response and *good try, not quite* for an incorrect one). Your response will prompt the children to say the correct final line together. If the answer is correct, discuss different methods of reaching the solution. If not, encourage the children to support each other to find the answer.

mental arithmetic

Song melodies

1 Three around the world – *Goosey goosey gander*

We can count in Eng - lish, you__ and__ me, Sing all to - ge - ther, one,__ two,__ three.

2 Food I like – *Chant*

Food I like, One, two, three, Chi - cken, cheese and cher - ry pie Taste good to me.

3 Five wonky bicycles – *John Brown's body*

One won - ky bi - cy - cle went rid - ing round the town, One won - ky bi - cy - cle went

rid - ing round the town, One won - ky bi - cy - cle went rid - ing round the town, Then

called a - no - ther bike to cy - cle round. *Solo:* San - - jay, fol - low on be -

- hind me, San - - jay, fol - low on be - hind me, San - - jay,

fol - low on be - hind me, We'll go 'bring, bring' as we ride a - round.

4 Five little seeds – *Here we go round the mulberry bush*

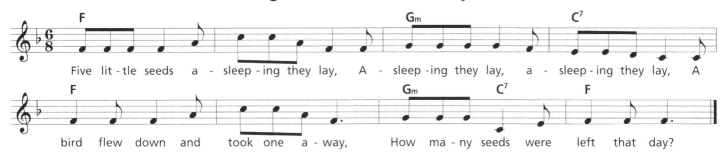

Five lit-tle seeds a - sleep-ing they lay, A - sleep-ing they lay, a - sleep-ing they lay, A
bird flew down and took one a - way, How ma-ny seeds were left that day?

5 One banana – One button (adapted)

One ba-na-na, two ba-na-nas, three ba-na-nas, four, Five ba-na-nas,
six ba-na-nas, se-ven ba-na-nas, more. Se-ven ba-na-nas, six ba-na-nas,
five ba-na-nas, four, Three ba-na-nas, two ba-na-nas, one, no more!

6 Five buzzy bees – *Once I caught a fish alive*

One, two, three, four, five, Bees come buzz-ing from the hive,
Six, se-ven, eight, nine, ten, Buzz a-round then back a-gain.

7 Mary up in a spaceship – *Mary, Mary, quite contrary*

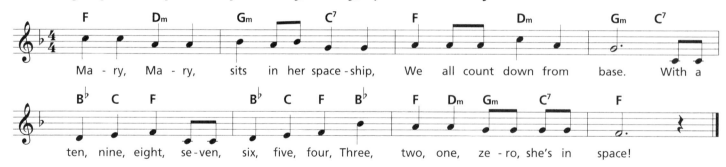

Ma - ry, Ma - ry, sits in her space - ship, We all count down from base. With a

ten, nine, eight, se - ven, six, five, four, Three, two, one, ze - ro, she's in space!

8 Hickory digital clock – *Hickory dickory dock*

Hi - cko - ry di - cko - ry dock, I am a di - gi - tal clock, When you're as - leep I

start to bleep, *Bleep, bleep, bleep,* What is the time on the clock?

9 Stamp and clap – *Polly put the kettle on*

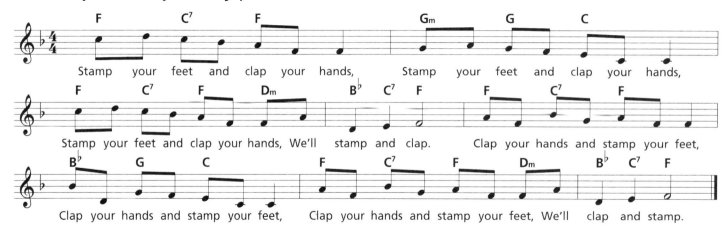

Stamp your feet and clap your hands, Stamp your feet and clap your hands,

Stamp your feet and clap your hands, We'll stamp and clap. Clap your hands and stamp your feet,

Clap your hands and stamp your feet, Clap your hands and stamp your feet, We'll clap and stamp.

10 Piggy pairs – *Tommy Thumb*

Pig-gy pairs, pig-gy pairs, Where are you? Here we are, here we are, How do you do?

11 Greedy crocodile – *What shall we do with the drunken sailor?*

I am a gree-dy cro-co-dile,— Spark-ling teeth and charm-ing smile,—

Come too near and in a while,— You will be my din-ner! One, two, three, four, five,—

One, two, three, four, five,— One, two, three, SNAP, SNAP,— Now I've had my din-ner!

12 Cherries on a plate – *The farmer's in his den*

Cher-ries on a plate, Cher-ries on a plate, Two,— four,— six,— eight,— Cher-ries on a plate.

13 Babies in their cots – *Jelly on a plate*

Ba-bies in their cots, Ba-bies in their cots, One, two, three, four, five, six, seven, eight, Ba-bies in their cots.

14 One, two, three, together – *In and out the dusky bluebells*

One, two, three, to-ge-ther, One, two, three, to-ge-ther, One, two, three, to-ge-ther, Clap your hands to-ge-ther.

15 Baa baa maths sheep – Baa baa black sheep (adapted)

Baa baa maths sheep, have you a-ny wool? Yes sir, yes sir, three bags full; One for the mas-ter, one for the dame, And one for the lit-tle boy who lives down the lane.

16 Bim bam bam – *Pat-a-cake*

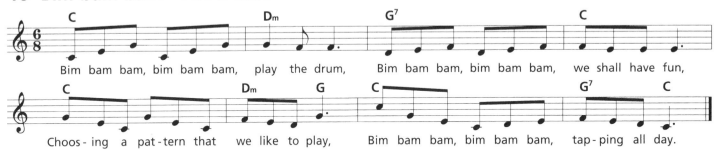

Bim bam bam, bim bam bam, play the drum, Bim bam bam, bim bam bam, we shall have fun, Choos-ing a pat-tern that we like to play, Bim bam bam, bim bam bam, tap-ping all day.

17 Ten little snowfriends – *Chant*

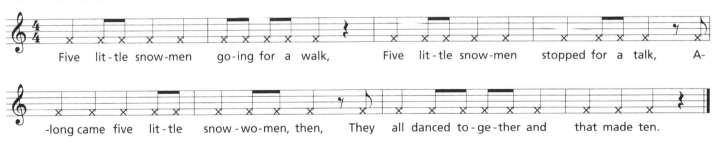

Five lit-tle snow-men go-ing for a walk, Five lit-tle snow-men stopped for a talk, A-long came five lit-tle snow-wo-men, then, They all danced to-ge-ther and that made ten.

18 The minibeast parade – The ants came marching (adapted)

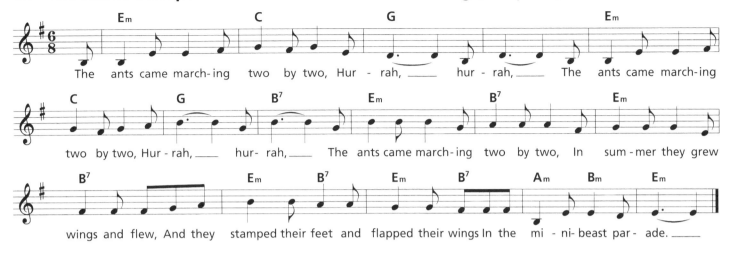

The ants came march-ing two by two, Hur - rah, _____ hur - rah, _____ The ants came march-ing two by two, Hur - rah, _____ hur - rah, _____ The ants came march-ing two by two, In sum - mer they grew wings and flew, And they stamped their feet and flapped their wings In the mi - ni - beast par - ade. _____

19 Centipede and millipede – *Jack and Jill*

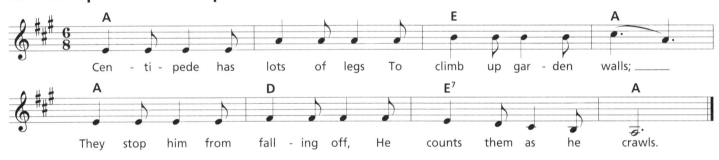

Cen - ti - pede has lots of legs To climb up gar - den walls; _____ They stop him from fall - ing off, He counts them as he crawls.

20 Circle – *Round and round the garden like a teddy bear*

Round and round the cir - cle, Draw one in the air, Stop, look, find one, Cir-cles are eve-ry-where.

21 Triangle – *Three blind mice*

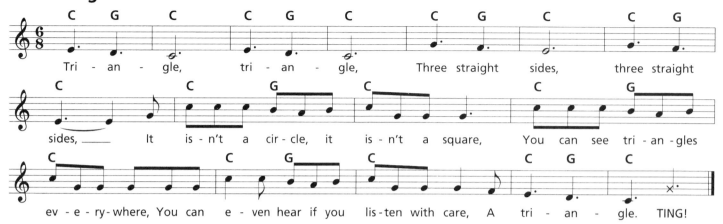

Tri - an - gle, tri - an - gle, Three straight sides, three straight

sides, ____ It is - n't a cir - cle, it is - n't a square, You can see tri - an - gles

ev - e - ry - where, You can e - ven hear if you lis - ten with care, A tri - an - gle. TING!

22 Square – *Frère Jacques*

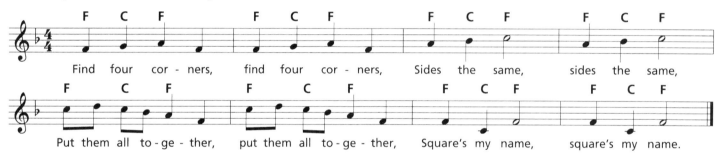

Find four cor - ners, find four cor - ners, Sides the same, sides the same,

Put them all to - ge - ther, put them all to - ge - ther, Square's my name, square's my name.

23 Which shapes? – *Oranges and lemons*

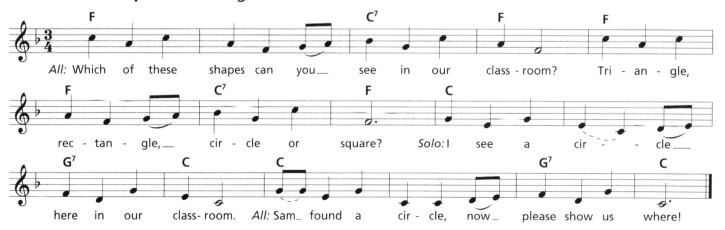

All: Which of these shapes can you_ see in our class - room? Tri - an - gle,

rec - tan - gle, _ cir - cle or square? *Solo:* I see a cir - cle _

here in our class - room. *All:* Sam _ found a cir - cle, now _ please show us where!

24 Sea shapes – *A sailor went to sea*

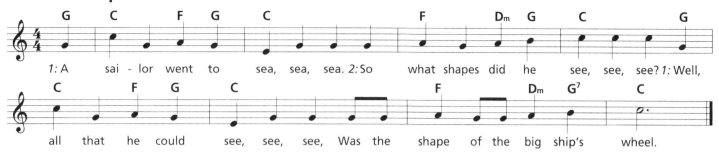

1: A sai - lor went to sea, sea, sea. *2:* So what shapes did he see, see, see? *1:* Well,

all that he could see, see, see, Was the shape of the big ship's wheel.

25 Mystery bag – *This old man*

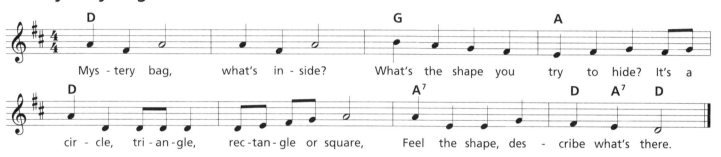

Mys - tery bag, what's in - side? What's the shape you try to hide? It's a

cir - cle, tri - an -gle, rec -tan - gle or square, Feel the shape, des - cribe what's there.

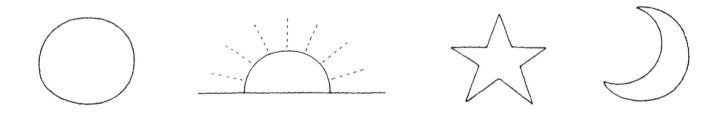

26 Sun, stars and moon – *Pease pudding hot*

Start of the day, Sun ris -ing high, Cir - cle of yel -low light In the sky.

27 Three ducks – *Twinkle, twinkle, little star*

Watch the ducks and you will see, They are wadd-ling, one, two, three.
First the small-est leads the line, Mid-dle-sized duck thinks se-cond place is fine,
Big-gest duck is third, you see, They are wadd-ling, one, two, three.

28 Favourite toys – *The wheels on the bus*

A yo-yo on a string rolls up and down, Up and down, up and down, A
yo-yo on a string rolls up and down, That's my fa-vou-rite toy.

29 The hokey cokey (adapted)

You put your right arm up, You put your right arm down, Up, down, up, down,
Shake it all a-round; You do the ho-key co-key And you turn a-round,____

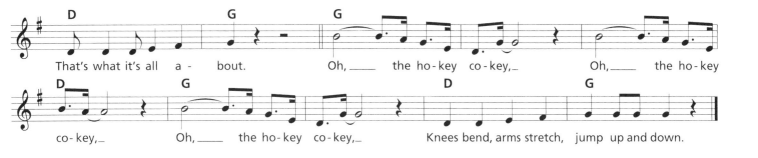

That's what it's all a - bout.   Oh, ___ the ho-key co-key,_   Oh,___ the ho-key

co-key,_   Oh, ___ the ho-key co-key,_   Knees bend, arms stretch, jump up and down.

30 Footsteps – The grand old Duke of York (adapted)

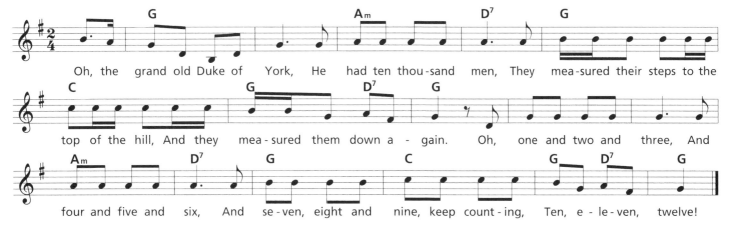

Oh, the grand old Duke of York, He had ten thou-sand men, They mea-sured their steps to the

top of the hill, And they mea-sured them down a - gain. Oh, one and two and three, And

four and five and six, And se-ven, eight and nine, keep count-ing, Ten, e - le-ven, twelve!

31 Recipes – *Yankee Doodle*

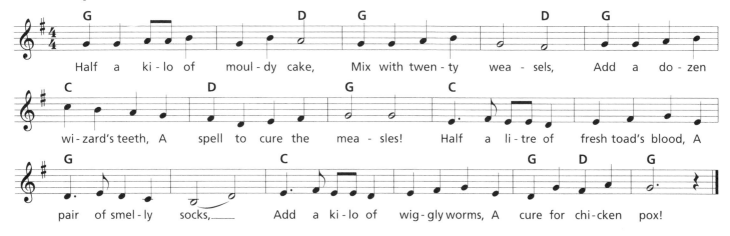

Half a ki-lo of moul-dy cake, Mix with twen-ty wea-sels, Add a do-zen

wi-zard's teeth, A spell to cure the mea-sles! Half a li-tre of fresh toad's blood, A

pair of smel-ly socks,___ Add a ki-lo of wig-gly worms, A cure for chi-cken pox!

32 Supermarket shop – *One man went to mow*

Going to buy some food,   At the su-per-mar-ket,_   One tin of baked beans,   Put it in the bas-ket._

33 Calculator heads – *She'll be coming round the mountain*

We have   all got cal-cu-la-tors in our   heads,   We have   all got cal-cu-la-tors in our   heads,   We have

all got cal-cu-la-tors, _   all got cal-cu-la-tors, _   All got cal-cu-la-tors in our   heads.

34 Double dumplings – *Diddle diddle dumpling*

Dou-ble, dou-ble dump-ling,   come with me,   Have a slice of cake and a   cup   of tea.

Choose a num-ber,   you will see,   We can dou-ble num-bers   ea-si-ly.

35 Hippity hop – *Pop goes the weasel*

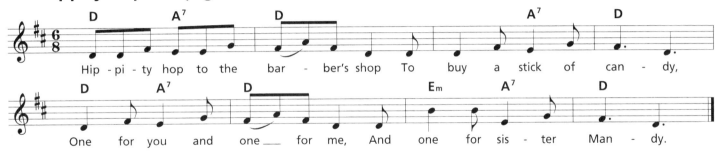

Hip - pi - ty hop to the bar - ber's shop To buy a stick of can - dy,

One for you and one for me, And one for sis - ter Man - dy.

36 Sing a song of pocket money – *Sing a song of sixpence*

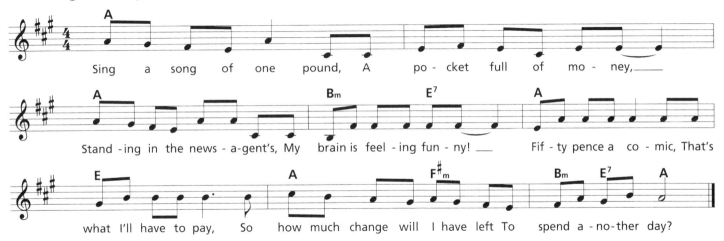

Sing a song of one pound, A po - cket full of mo - ney, ___

Stand - ing in the news - a - gent's, My brain is feel - ing fun - ny! ___ Fif - ty pence a co - mic, That's

what I'll have to pay, So how much change will I have left To spend a - no - ther day?

37 Tom Thumb – *Chant*

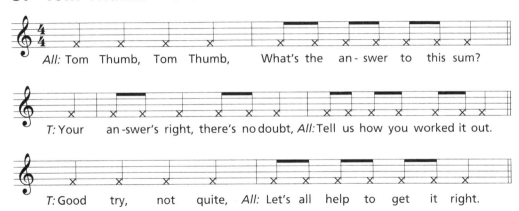

All: Tom Thumb, Tom Thumb, What's the an - swer to this sum?

T: Your an - swer's right, there's no doubt, *All:* Tell us how you worked it out.

T: Good try, not quite, *All:* Let's all help to get it right.

Song title and first line index

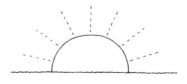